⑤ My numbers (pages 40–47)

Vocabulary	Chant: Grammar	Story and value	CLIL	
one, two, three, four	one book, two books	**Where's Polly?** Playing together	Quantity	Describing with numbers

▶ **Total physical response:** Four, three, two, one   ▶ **Song: Sing some more**

⑥ My pets (pages 48–55)

Vocabulary	Chant: Grammar	Story and value	CLIL	Thinking skills
bird, rabbit, fish, cat	What is it?	**The cat** Working as a team	Species	Making deductions

▶ **Total physical response:** Jump, walk, fly, swim   ▶ **Song: What is this?**

⑦ My food (pages 56–63)

Vocabulary	Chant: Grammar	Story and value	CLIL	Thinking skills
pasta, salad, rice, cake	I like (rice).	**The cake** Sharing	Solids and liquids	Focusing on detail

▶ **Total physical response:** Look! Pasta, eat the pasta, it's lovely, wash your face   ▶ **Song: I like lovely lunch!**

⑧ My clothes (pages 64–71)

Vocabulary	Chant: Grammar	Story and value	CLIL	Thinking skills
T-shirt, trousers, dress, shoes	I don't like (the purple dress).	**The party** Including your friends	Dressing up	Categorising

▶ **Total physical response:** Put on the shoes, put on a T-shirt, put on a hat, say 'hello' to your dad   ▶ **Song: Clothes**

⑨ My park (pages 72–79)

Vocabulary	Chant: Grammar	Story and value	CLIL	Thinking skills
slide, roundabout, seesaw, swing	The (swing)'s fun.	**The park** Taking turns	Circles and triangles	Sequencing

▶ **Total physical response:** Sit down on the seesaw, down you go, up you go, oh no   ▶ **Song: Let's go to the park**

Phonics (pages 80–89)

Unit 1: 'p' pencil	Unit 2: 'b' bag	Unit 3: 'd' dad	Unit 4: 'c' car	Unit 5: 't' two	Unit 6: 'e' eggs	Unit 7: 's' salad	Unit 8: 'n' nose	Unit 9: 'i' igloo	Phonics review

Review **pages 90–94**   **Certificate:** 95   **Stickers:** End section

 www.cambridge.org/supersafari/familyfun

Hello!

Listen and point. Say the names.

3 lly, Leo, Mike

2 Listen and chant.

Family fun!

Hello! I'm (Jo).

1

2

3

1 My class

1 CD1 08 **Listen and point. Say the words.**

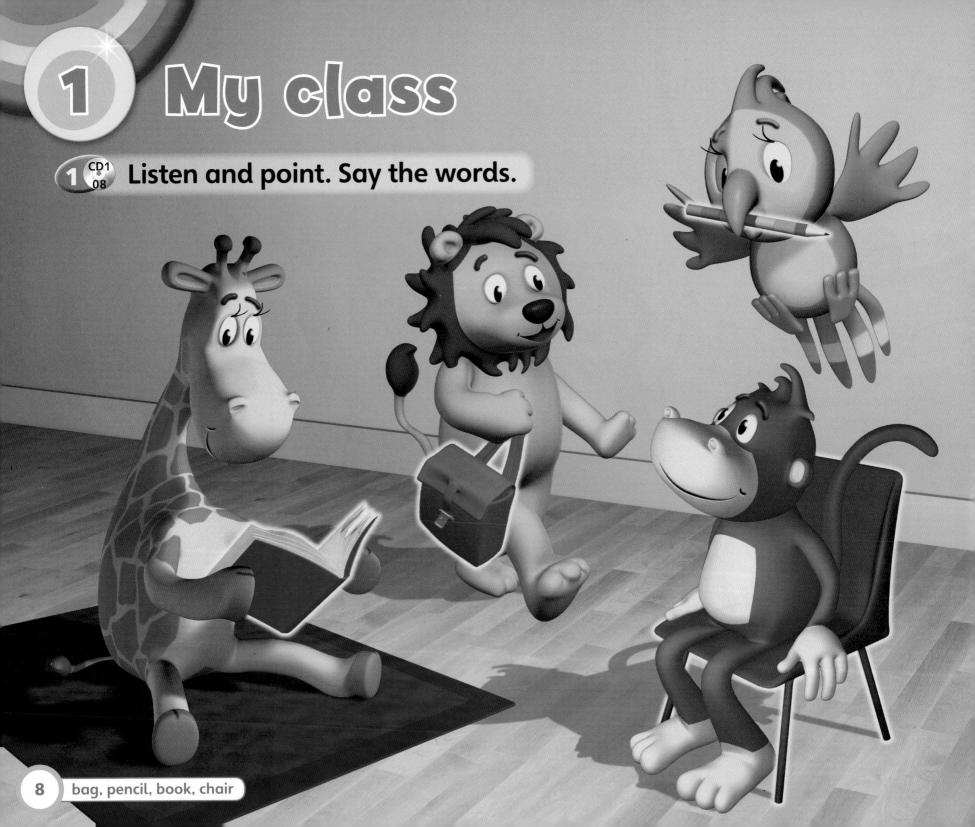

8 | bag, pencil, book, chair

2 CD1 09 **Listen and trace. Chant.**

1

2

3

4

3 Listen and act.

4 CD1 13 14 **Listen and sing.**

1

The chair

1

2

3

4

Value: Saying *sorry*

13

School behaviour

6 CD1 17 Listen and point. Say the words.

7 (Think!) **Look and complete the faces.**

1

2

Thinking skills: Classifying   **15**

2 My colours

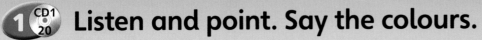

1 Listen and point. Say the colours.

16 red, blue, green, yellow

2 CD1 21 Listen and colour. Chant.

3 CD1 22 23 **Listen and act. Listen and colour.**

1

2

3

The painters

Values

20 Story

Rainbow colours

6 CD1 30 **Listen and point. Say the colours.**

7 Think! Look and say the colours. Colour.

1

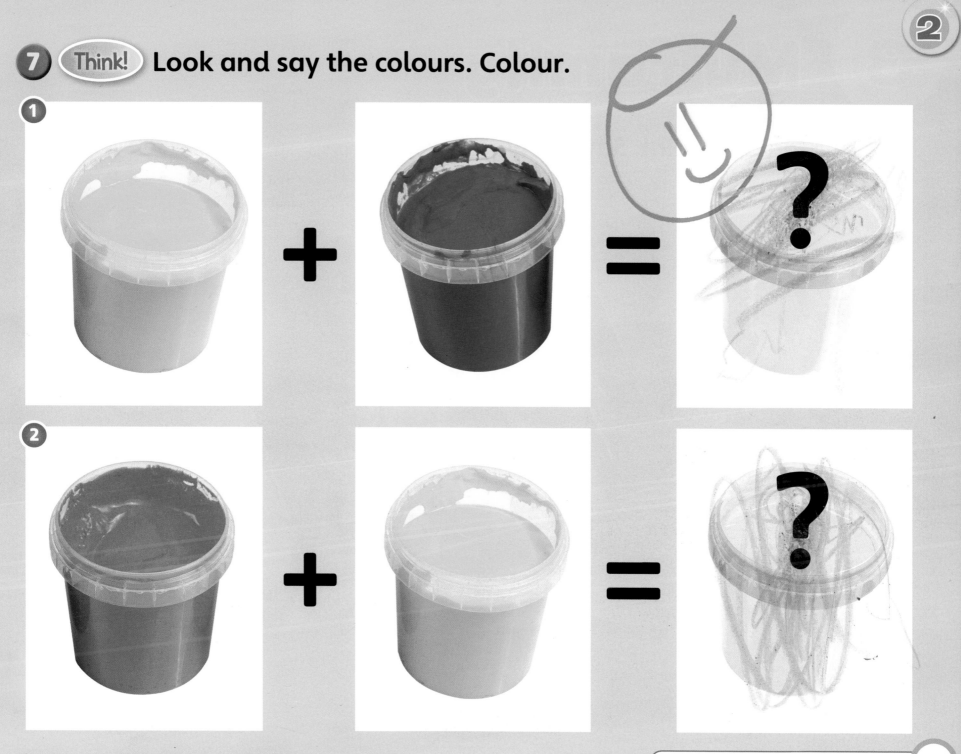

Thinking skills: Testing predictions   23

③ My family

1 CD1 32 **Listen and point. Say the words.**

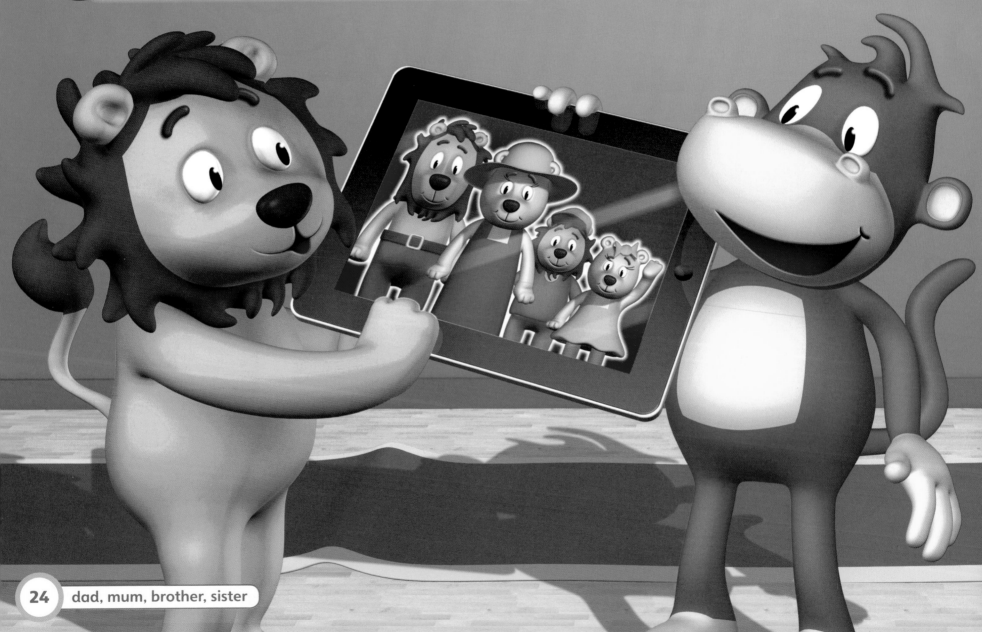

dad, mum, brother, sister

2 CD1 33 **Listen and trace. Chant.**

1

2

3

4

 Who's this? 25

Listen and act. Listen and colour.

CD1
34 35

①

②

③

4 CD1 37 38 **Listen and sing.**

Family fun!

Family and friends

1

2

3

4

Animal families

Listen and point. Trace and say the words.

7 **Think!** **Follow the path.**

Thinking skills: Ordering **31**

4 My toys

1 CD1 45 **Listen and point. Say the toys.**

32 ball, car, puzzle, doll

2 Listen and match. Chant.

CD1 47

1

2

3

3 Listen and act. Listen and colour.

CD1 48 49

1

2

3

4

Listen and sing.

The puzzle

1

2

3

4

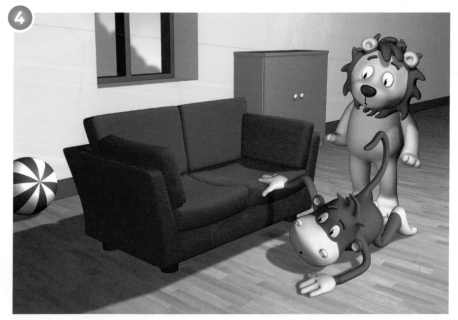

Value: Helping

Big and small

6 CD1 56 Listen and point. Trace and say the words.

① ② ③ ④ ⑤ ⑥

7 Think! **Look and draw lines. Say 'big' or 'small'.**

1

2

3

4

5

6

5 My numbers

 Listen and point. Say the numbers.

2 CD2 04 **Listen and match. Chant.**

1

2

3

4

 : ⋮

 ·

 ·

 ⋮

Family fun!

one book, two books 41

CD2 05 06 # Listen and act. Listen and colour.

Total physical response

4 CD2 08 09 **Listen and sing.**

Where's Polly?

1

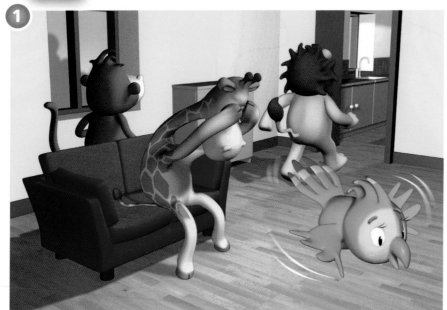

2

3

4

Quantity

6 🔘 **CD2 13** Listen and point. Trace and say the numbers.

1

2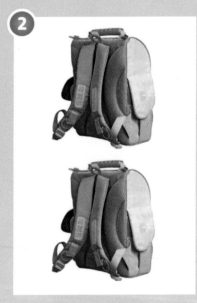

3

4

7 (Think!) **Look and match. Say the numbers.**

1 2 3 4

Thinking skills: Describing with numbers **47**

6 My pets

1 CD2 16 **Listen and point. Say the pets.**

bird, rabbit, fish, cat

2 **CD2** **17** **Listen and colour. Chant.**

Family fun! What is it? 49

3 CD2 19 20 Listen and act. Listen and colour.

1

2

3

4

4 CD2 22 23 **Listen and sing.**

Family fun!

Value: Working as a team

Species

6 CD2 8 26 **Listen and point. Draw lines and say.**

7 (Think!) **Look and say the words.**

1

2

3

4
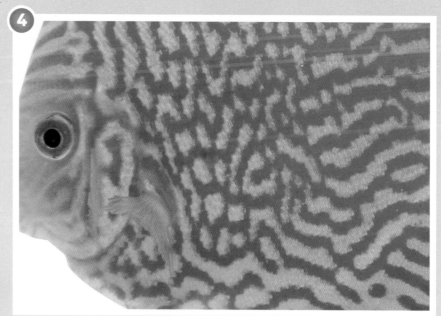

7 My food

1 _{CD2 28} **Listen and point. Say the food.**

56 pasta, salad, rice, cake

2 CD2 8 29 Listen and trace. Chant.

1

2

3

4

4 CD2 33 34 **Listen and sing.**

1

2

3

4

Solids and liquids

6 CD2 37 **Listen and point. Trace and say the food.**

1

2

3

4

7 Think! **Look and match.**

1

2

3

4

8 My clothes

1 CD2 40 **Listen and point. Say the clothes.**

T-shirt, trousers, dress, shoes

2 Listen and colour. Chant.

Family fun!   I don't like (the purple dress).   65

3 **Listen and act. Listen and colour.**

CD2 43 44

1

2

3

4

4 CD2 46 47 **Listen and sing.**

The party

1

2

3

4

Value: Including your friends

Dressing up

6 CD2 50 **Listen and point. Trace and say the words.**

①

②

③

7 Think! **Circle the clothes.**

Thinking skills: Categorising   **71**

⑨ My park

1 CD2 52 **Listen and point. Say the words.**

slide, roundabout, seesaw, swing

2 Listen and match. Chant.

CD2 54

1

2

3

4

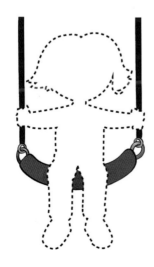

Family fun!

The (swing)'s fun. **73**

3 **CD2** 56 57 **Listen and act. Listen and colour.**

1

2

3

4

4 CD2 59 60 **Listen and sing.**

The park

Circles and triangles

6 **CD2** **63** Listen and point. Count and say the shapes.

7 **Think!** **Look and draw lines. Say the shapes.**

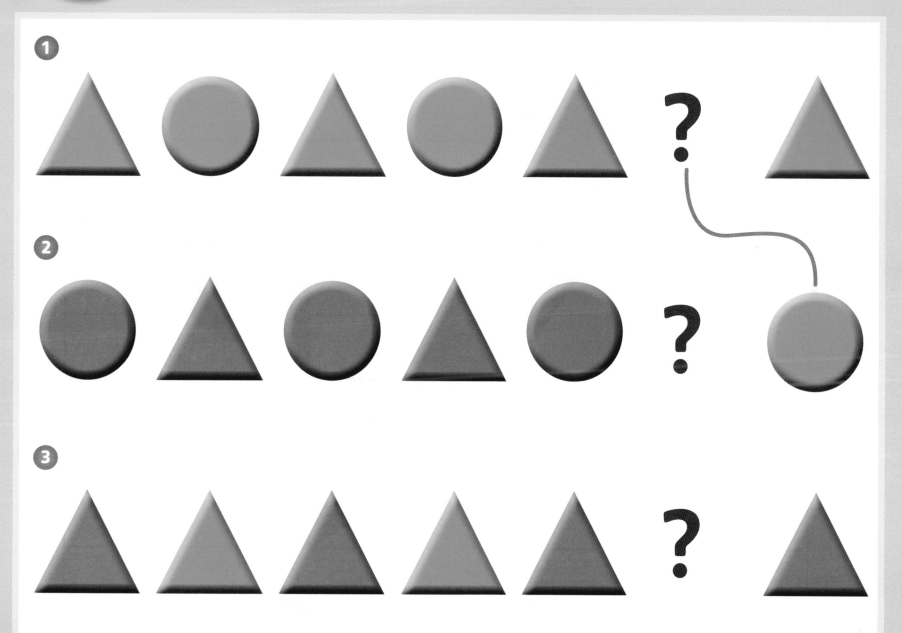

1 Look and find.

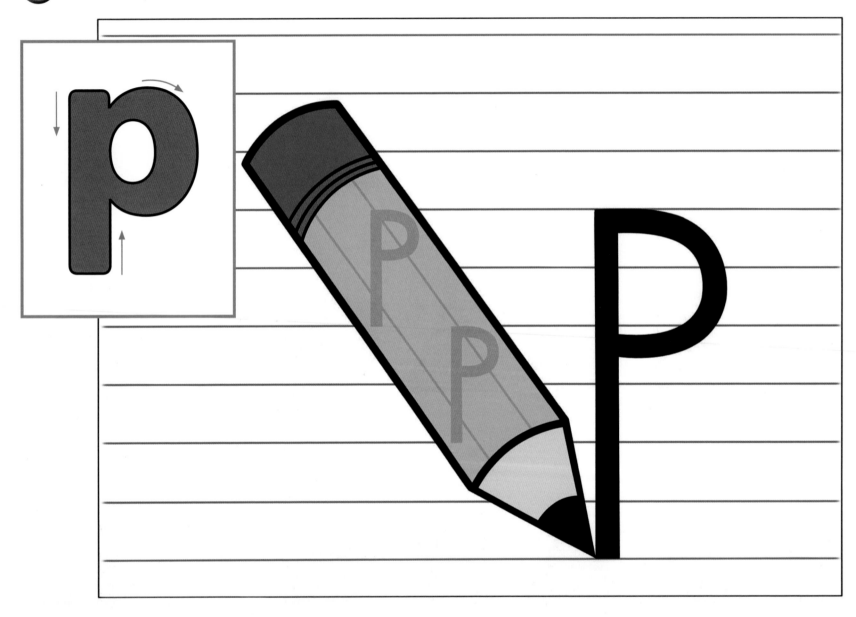

1 Look and find.

Phonics

2 Listen and join in.

Unit 2: 'b' bag 81

1 Look and find.

1 Look and find. Colour the letter.

2 CD1 57 Listen and join in.

1 Look and find. Colour the letter.

2 CD2 8 14 Listen and join in.

1 Look and find. Colour the letter.

2 Listen and join in.

1 Look and find. Trace the letter.

1 Look and find. Trace the letter.

2 CD2 51 Listen and join in.

1 Look and find. Trace the letter.

2 CD2 64 Listen and join in.

1 CD2 66 **Listen and play bingo.**

1 Listen to the sentences. Colour the frames.

1

Listen and colour the circles. Colour the frames.

1 Listen and colour the circles. Colour the frames.

1 Listen and colour the circles. Colour the frames.

CD2
8
65

....

has finished Super Safari!

Thanks and acknowledgements

Authors' thanks

The authors would like to thank a number of people who have made significant contributions towards the final form of Super Safari: Colin Sage, Helen Brock and Carolyn Wright, our editors, for their expertise in working on the manuscripts, and the support we got from them.

Our designers, Blooberry, for their imaginative layout and all the artists – in particular Bill Bolton – for the inspiring artwork that has brought our ideas to life in such beautiful ways.

Liane Grainger, Managing Editor and Emily Hird, Publisher, for their many useful suggestions for improvement.

Jason Mann, Editorial Director at Cambridge University Press, for his vision and encouragement.

The publishers are grateful to the following contributors:

Blooberry Design: cover design, book design and page make-up
Bill Bolton: cover illustration
Alison Prior: picture research
Ian Harker: audio recording and production
James Richardson: chant writing and production
Robert Lee, Dib Dib Dub Studios: song writing and production

The publishers and authors are grateful to the following illustrators:

Bill Bolton; Judy Brown; Gareth Conway (The Bright Agency); Kate Daubney; Mark Duffin; Louise Garner; Sue King (Plum Pudding Illustration); Bernice Lum

The authors and publishers acknowledge the following sources of copyright material and are grateful for the permissions granted. While every effort has been made, it has not always been possible to identify the sources of all the material used, or to trace all copyright holders. If any omissions are brought to our notice, we will be happy to include the appropriate acknowledgements on reprinting.

The publishers are grateful to the following for permission to reproduce copyright photographs and material:

p.14 (TL): Shutterstock/© Ermolaev Alexander; p.14 (BL): Shutterstock/© Nina Buday; p.14 (R): Shutterstock/© Rawpixel; p.23 (all): Shutterstock/© Mathias Rosenthal; p.30 (L): Shutterstock/© Svetland Foote; p.30 (R): Shutterstock/© Kharkhan Oleg; p.30 (BR): Alamy/© Peter Stone; p.30 (BC): Shutterstock/© Irin-K;p.31 (BR): Shutterstock/© IT Studio; p.31 (BL): Shutterstock/© Volodymyr Burdak; p.31 (TR): Shutterstock/© Irin-K; p.31 (TL): Shutterstock/© HardHeadMonster; p.38 (TR): Shutterstock/© Jocic; p.38 (BR): Shutterstock/© Andy Piatt; p.38 (TC): Alamy/© Superstock; p.38 (BC): Shutterstock/© Home Studio; p.38 (TL): Alamy/© Oleksiy Maksyrenko; p.38 (BL): Shutterstock/© graja; p.39 (TL): Shutterstock/© Pavla; p.39 (TR): Shutterstock/© naluwan; p.39 (CL): Alamy/© Fine Art; p.39 (CR): Getty Images/© Karen Ilagen; p.39 (BL): Shutterstock/© Martyn Novak; p.39 (BR): Getty Images/© Image Bank/ MoMo Productions; p.46 (I): Shutterstock/© ikphotographers; p.46 (2): Shutterstock/© diless; p.46 (3): Shutterstock/© Funny Solution Studio; p.46 (4): Shutterstock/© Zayats Svetlana; p.47 (I): Shutterstock/© Dan Thornberg; p.47 (2): Shutterstock/© Dean Harty; p.47 (3): Shutterstock/© Bestv; p.47 (4): Shutterstock/© Irina Rogova; p.54 (BC): Shutterstock/© Gillmar; p.54 (C): Shutterstock/© Butterfly Hunter; p.54 (CR): Shutterstock/© Tooykrub; p.54 (TC): Shutterstock/© Phasut Warapisit; p.54 (CL): Shutterstock/© Mexrix; p.54 (BL. TR): Shutterstock/© Erick Isselee; p.54 (BR): Shutterstock/© Aaron Amat; p.54 (TL): Shutterstock/© Marina Jay; p.55 (TL): Shutterstock/© Jiang Hongyan; p.55 (TR): Shutterstock/© Eric Isselee; p.55 (BL): Shutterstock/© Luck Luckyfarm;p.55 (BR): Shutterstock/© Nantatwat Chotsuwan; p.62 (TL): Shutterstock/© Natalia Mylova; p.62 (TR): Shutterstock/© Ksena2you; p.62 (BL): Shutterstock/© Pavlo Loushkin; p.62 (BR): Shutterstock/© Prapass; p.70 (L): Shutterstock/© Irinak; p.70 (C): Alamy/© Radius Images; p.70 (R): Shutterstock/© Andresr; p.71 (TL): Shutterstock/© Gemenacom; p.71 (TC): Shutterstock/© Roma Sigaev; p.71 (TR): Shutterstock/ © Munal Ozman; p.71 (CL): Shutterstock/© Maksym Bonderchuck; p.71 (C): Shutterstock/© Lucy Liu; p.71 (BC): Shutterstock/© Meelena; p.71 (BL): Shutterstock/© Coprid; p.71 (BR): Shutterstock/© Karkas.

UNIT 1
page 13

UNIT 2
page 21

UNIT 3
page 29

UNIT 4
page 37

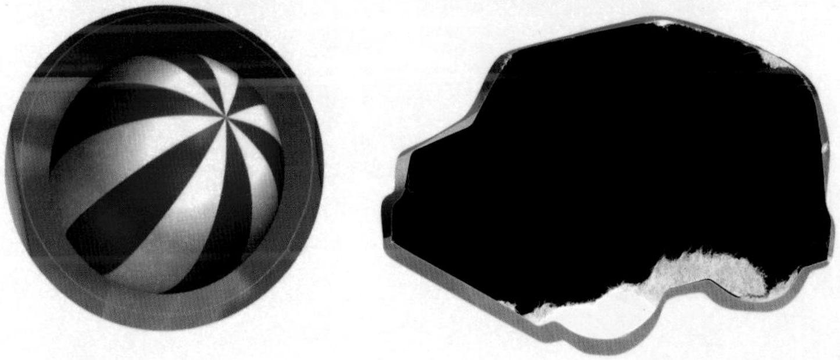

UNIT 5
page 45

FUN STICKERS

UNIT 7
page 61

UNIT 9
page 77